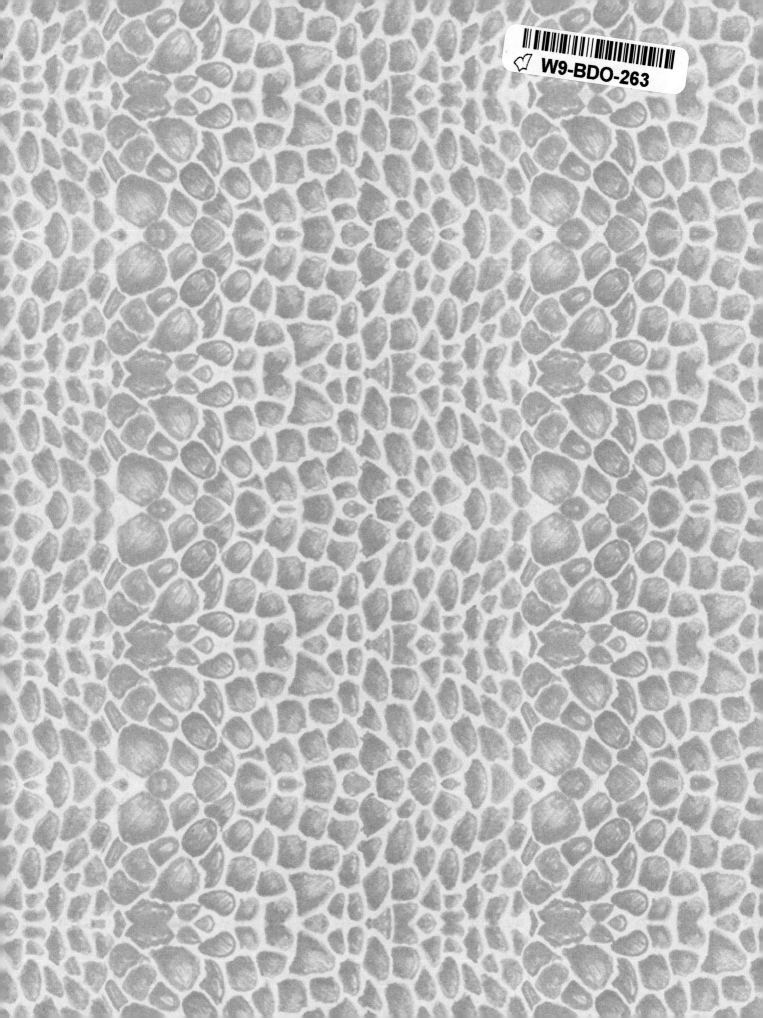

ENCYCLOPEDIA OF
DINOSAURS
AND OTHER PREHISTORIC CREATURES

This 2007 edition published by Backpack Books by arrangement with Parragon Publishing.

Designers

Julie Joubinaux, Rob Shone
Illustrators
Norma Burgin, Mark Dolby,
Graham Kennedy, Peter Komarnysky,
Damian Quayle, Neil Reed, Pete Roberts
(Allied Artists)
James Field, Terry Riley (SGA)
Mike Atkinson, Chris Forsey, Rob Shone
Editor
James Pickering

ISBN-13: 978-0-7607-4217-4
ISBN-10: 0-7607-4217-0

Printed and bound in China

5   7   9   10   8   6

ENCYCLOPEDIA OF DINOSAURS
AND OTHER PREHISTORIC CREATURES

JOHN MALAM & STEVE PARKER

BACK**PACK** BOOKS
∘
NEW YORK

CONTENTS

CHAPTER ONE
ANCESTORS OF THE DINOSAURS

WHAT ARE REPTILES?
12

THE ORIGIN OF REPTILES
14

AMPHIBIANS 1
16

AMPHIBIANS 2
18

ACANTHOSTEGA
20

THE FIRST REPTILES ON LAND 1
22

THE FIRST REPTILES ON LAND 2
24

THE FIRST REPTILES ON LAND 3
26

HYLONOMUS
28

PELYCOSAURS AND MAMMAL-LIKE REPTILES
30

MAMMAL-LIKE REPTILES 1
32

MAMMAL-LIKE REPTILES 2
34

THE PERMIAN MASS EXTINCTION
36

MAMMAL-LIKE REPTILES 3
38

CHAPTER TWO
KILLERS AND SCAVENGERS

THEROPODS – THE MEAT-EATERS
42

THE FIRST MEAT-EATERS
44

LARGE-SIZED MEAT-EATERS 1
46

LARGE-SIZED MEAT-EATERS 2
48

Tyrannosaurus Rex
50
Spinosaurs
52
Baryonyx
54
Miscellaneous meat-eaters
56
Oviraptor
58
Ornithomimids
60
Dromaeosaurs
62
Deinonychus
64
"Dino-birds" 1
66
"Dino-birds" 2
68

CHAPTER THREE
GIANT PLANT-EATING DINOSAURS

Sauropods – the giant plant-eaters
72
Prosauropods 1
74
Prosauropods 2
76
Massospondylus
78
Cetiosaurs
80
Camarasaurs
82
Brachiosaurus
84
Diplodocids 1
86
Diplodocids 2
88

DIPLODOCUS
90
TITANOSAURS 1
92
TITANOSAURS 2
94
TITANOSAURS 3
96
TITANOSAURUS
98

CHAPTER FOUR
ARMOR, HORNS AND PLATES

PLATED, ARMORED, HORNED AND
BONE-HEADED DINOSAURS
102
PLATED DINOSAURS – STEGOSAURS 1
104
PLATED DINOSAURS – STEGOSAURS 2
106
PLATED DINOSAURS – STEGOSAURS 3
108

STEGOSAURUS
110
ARMORED DINOSAURS – THE NODOSAURS
112
ARMORED DINOSAURS – THE ANKYLOSAURS
114
ANKYLOSAURUS
116
HORNED DINOSAURS – CERATOPSIANS 1
118
HORNED DINOSAURS – CERATOPSIANS 2
120
TRICERATOPS
122
BONE-HEADED DINOSAURS –
PACHYCEPHALOSAURS 1
124
BONE-HEADED DINOSAURS –
PACHYCEPHALOSAURS 2
126
STEGOCERAS
128

CHAPTER FIVE
DUCK-BILLS AND OTHER DINOSAURS

ORNITHOPODS – THE "BIRD-FEET" DINOSAURS
132
HETERODONTOSAURS 1
134
HETERODONTOSAURS 2
136
LESOTHOSAURUS
138
HYPSILOPHODONTS 1
140
HYPSILOPHODONTS 2
142
LEAELLYNASAURA
144
IGUANODONTS 1
146
IGUANODONTS 2
148
IGUANODON
150

HADROSAURS 1
152
HADROSAURS 2
154
HADROSAURS 3
156
MAIASAURA
158

CHAPTER SIX
PTEROSAURS

FLYING REPTILES OF THE DINOSAUR AGE
162
TRIASSIC PTEROSAURS
164
EUDIMORPHODON
166
JURASSIC PTEROSAURS OF EUROPE
168
DIMORPHODON
170
LATE JURASSIC PTEROSAURS
172

THE PTERODACTYLS ARRIVE
174
UNUSUAL JURASSIC PTEROSAURS
176
PTERODACTYLUS
178
EARLY CRETACEOUS PTEROSAURS
180
CRETACEOUS SPECIALIZED FEEDERS
182
FLYING ACROSS THE WORLD
184
PTEROSAUR HEYDAY
186
QUETZALCOATLUS
188

CHAPTER SEVEN
THE TEEMING SEAS

OCEANS IN THE AGE OF DINOSAURS
192
NOTHOSAURS
194
PLESIOSAURS
196
ELASMOSAURUS
198
PLIOSAURS
200
LIOPLEURODON
202
RISE OF THE ICHTHYOSAURS
204
ICHTHYOSAUR MYSTERIES
206
ICHTHYOSAURUS
208
MOSASAURS
210

MOSASAURUS
212
TURTLES AND PLACODONTS
214
ARCHELON
216
SHARKS
218

CHAPTER EIGHT
THE WORLD OF THE DINOSAURS

HISTORY OF THE EARTH
222
THE TRIASSIC PERIOD
224
THE JURASSIC PERIOD
226
THE CRETACEOUS PERIOD
228

DINOSAUR SKELETONS
230
DINOSAUR MUSCLES AND ORGANS
232
DINOSAUR FAMILY TREE
234
HOW FOSSILS ARE FORMED
236
THE HISTORY OF DINOSAUR-HUNTING
238
DIGGING FOR DINOSAURS
240
DISPLAYING DINOSAURS
242
DEATH OF THE DINOSAURS 1
244
DEATH OF THE DINOSAURS 2
246
AFTER THE DINOSAURS
248

GLOSSARY
250
INDEX
254

CHAPTER ONE

ANCESTORS OF THE DINOSAURS

Life first appeared on Earth about 3.8 billion years ago. From the first simple life-forms that lived in the sea, life gradually moved on to the land, and into the sky. Life learned how to survive in Earth's different habitats. Within each habitat were groups of animals specially adapted to live there. One group of animals that became very successful was the reptiles.

REPTILE CHARACTERISTICS
Reptiles are animals with backbones – they are vertebrates. They lay hard-shelled eggs, have scaly skin, and are cold-blooded (their bodies are the same temperature as their surroundings).

Dinosaurs were the largest reptiles on land.

When dinosaurs were alive, Earth was very different from the world we know today. This scene shows a landscape from about 100 million years ago. It was a time when the first flowering plants appeared, and when oak, maple, walnut and beech trees grew alongside conifers, cycads and ferns.

WHEN REPTILES RULED THE EARTH
At one time, long ago in the prehistoric past, reptiles were the most successful animals alive. The time in which they ruled the Earth is called the Mesozoic Era. It lasted for about 185 million years, starting 250 million years ago and ending 65 million years ago. Mesozoic means "middle life." It refers to an era mid-way between two other eras – the Palaeozoic ("ancient life") and our own Cenozoic ("recent life").

PREHISTORIC REPTILES

In the Mesozoic Era reptiles dominated the land, the sea, and the sky. Other groups of animals, such as mammals, fish and insects, lived alongside them. Because reptiles were so successful during the Mesozoic Era, this time of Earth's history is also known as the Age of Reptiles. Sea-living swimming reptiles belonged to a group known as the plesiosaurs. Sky-living flying reptiles belonged to a group known as the pterosaurs. And as for the reptiles that lived on the land, they are the best-known of all – the dinosaurs.

While dinosaurs roamed across the land, their reptile cousins commanded the sky and the sea. Fast-flying pterosaurs flew on leathery wings, and streamlined plesiosaurs, pliosaurs and fish-like ichthyosaurs ruled the sea.

MODERN REPTILES

After the Mesozoic Era ended, 65 million years ago, a new time in Earth's history began – our own era, in which mammals are the dominant animal group. Many reptile species, including dinosaurs, did not survive into this new age. However, some did, such as crocodiles, lizards, turtles and snakes.

There are nearly 6,000 different kinds of reptiles living on Earth today.

THE ORIGIN OF REPTILES

The world's first reptiles appeared about 300 million years ago. These new kinds of creatures evolved from an older group of animals, known as amphibians.

LIVING A DOUBLE LIFE

The word amphibian means "double life," and describes a group of animals that can live both in water and on land. Amphibians were the first vertebrates to develop legs with feet, not fins. Their feet enabled them to move on the ground, and because their feet were webbed, they could also swim. Although they could survive on land, amphibians still had to spend some of their time in water. Like frogs and newts today, early amphibians laid their soft, jelly-covered eggs in water. But in order to live entirely on land, big changes had to happen in their bodies and their way of life.

LEAVING THE WATER

For ancient amphibians there were disadvantages to their watery way of life. Their young – tadpoles – were born in water, and many would have been eaten by predators, such as fish and water scorpions. Adult amphibians faced this danger, too. For more of them to survive, amphibians had to learn how to live entirely on dry land.

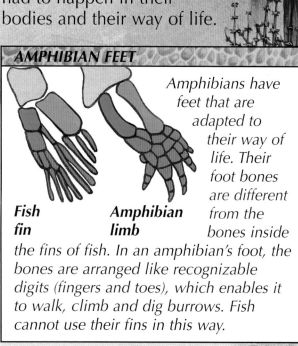

AMPHIBIAN FEET

Fish fin

Amphibian limb

Amphibians have feet that are adapted to their way of life. Their foot bones are different from the bones inside the fins of fish. In an amphibian's foot, the bones are arranged like recognizable digits (fingers and toes), which enables it to walk, climb and dig burrows. Fish cannot use their fins in this way.

LIVING ON DRY LAND

Two big changes helped amphibians to live entirely on dry land. Over a long time, their thin, smooth skin thickened and became covered in scales. This new type of skin stopped their bodies from drying out. Also, they began to lay eggs with hard shells. Their young hatched on to land, not into water. These were the world's first reptiles.

MODERN AMPHIBIANS

There are more than 4,200 species of amphibian on Earth today. They are divided into three groups – frogs and toads, newts and salamanders, and worm-like caecilians (found in tropical regions). They range in size from tiny frogs just one third of an inch (1cm) long, to salamanders that grow to 5ft (1.5m) in length.

Amphibians have lived on Earth for the last 350 million years. Like reptiles, mammals, fish and birds, they have backbones – but they can be separated from these other animal groups because they have moist, smooth skin without scales, hair or feathers. Amphibians were the world's first tetrapods – animals with four limbs. They evolved from fish that had fleshy, bony fins, known as lobes.

spent much of its time there. Instead, *Ichthyostega* may have developed its legs to help it clamber over plants which grew in the streams where it lived most of its life. Its short, stiff legs may only have had limited movement. To move on to land it may have hauled itself up by its forelegs while dragging its hindquarters.

EOGYRINUS

Carboniferous,
300 million years ago
Europe
15ft (4.6m) long

Eogyrinus

ICHTHYOSTEGA

Devonian, 370 mya
Greenland
5ft (1.5m) long
This creature is one of the world's first amphibians. Scientists describe it as a "four-legged fish" because it has a fish-like head, body and tail. Its four legs with webbed toes show that it could walk, which means it had adapted to life on land, though it may not have

One of the largest amphibians ever to have lived, *Eogyrinus* was a powerful swimmer that moved quickly through the water by swishing its long tail from side to side. It may have been a predator, lying in wait in the shallows, in much the same way as a crocodile does today. Although probably better suited to hunting in the water, *Eogyrinus* could probably make a grab for prey passing close by on the land.

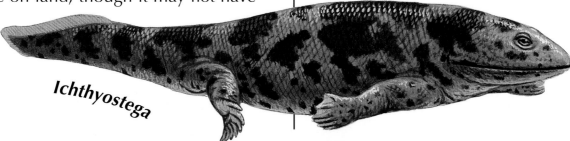

Ichthyostega

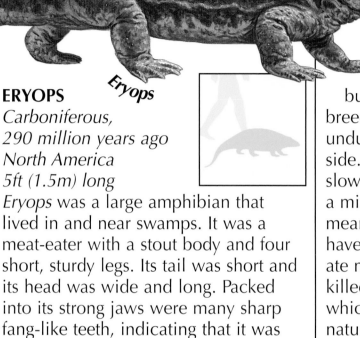

Eryops

SEYMOURIA

Permian, 280 mya
North America
2ft (60cm) long
Seymouria was a small animal that spent most of its time on land, like a reptile, but which returned to the water to breed, like an amphibian. It walked by undulating its backbone from side to side. Its short forelimbs show it was a slow mover. *Seymouria* may have had a mixed meat and plant diet, which means it was an omnivore. It may also have been a carrion-eater, meaning it ate meat from animals killed by others, or which had died of natural causes.

ERYOPS

Carboniferous,
290 million years ago
North America
5ft (1.5m) long
Eryops was a large amphibian that lived in and near swamps. It was a meat-eater with a stout body and four short, sturdy legs. Its tail was short and its head was wide and long. Packed into its strong jaws were many sharp fang-like teeth, indicating that it was probably a predatory animal. *Eryops* may have hunted for fish, giant cockroaches, millipedes, dragonflies, and smaller amphibians and reptiles.

Seymouria

Eryops *was one of the first true four-legged animals on Earth, able to walk on land. However, it was not a good walker. Its legs had to lift its heavy body clear of the ground, but because they were only short they could not raise it very high. When* Eryops *moved it probably dragged its belly on the ground. With this sprawling body posture,* Eryops *could only take short, broad strides. Its walk was slow and difficult, and it probably could not run.* Eryops *may have been a slow, ungainly mover on land, but when it returned to the water it might have been a good swimmer.*

A great variety of amphibians existed in the time before reptiles became the most dominant animals on Earth. Each species of amphibian evolved its own unique features, such as the gills of the adult *Gerrothorax*.

Diplocaulus

DIPLOCAULUS
Permian, 270 mya
North America
3ft 3in (1m) long
With a body shaped like that of a modern salamander, the amphibian *Diplocaulus* had an unusual triangular-shaped head. The "wings" on either side of its head might have streamlined its shape, helping it to glide through the water. They might have been a safety feature, making it hard for predators to swallow *Diplocaulus*. Also, because they made the head seem large, they might have frightened some predators away.

MASTODONSAURUS
Triassic, 230 mya
Europe, Africa
13ft (4m) long
Mastodonsaurus was an enormous amphibian with a short body and

tail, and a massive, flat skull. In a fully-grown adult the skull could be 5ft (1.5m) long. Its jaws were packed with many small, sharp teeth, and a pair of tusks pointed up from its lower jaw and through openings in the upper jaw. It is thought that *Mastodonsaurus* fed exclusively on fish, which it caught in the lakes, ponds and swamps where it lived.

Mastodonsaurus

PARACYCLOTOSAURUS

Triassic, 235 million years ago
Australia, India, South Africa
7ft 5in (2.3m) long
Paracyclotosaurus was a giant amphibian with a flat body, similar in looks to today's salamander – but much, much larger. Although it could live on dry land, *Paracyclotosaurus* probably spent most of its time in water. A fish-eater, it might have played a waiting game, lying just below the surface of the water. When an unsuspecting fish came within reach of its jaws, *Paracyclotosaurus* lifted its massive head, its mouth opened wide and the fish was sucked inside.

Modern predators, such as crocodiles, use this technique to catch some of their prey.

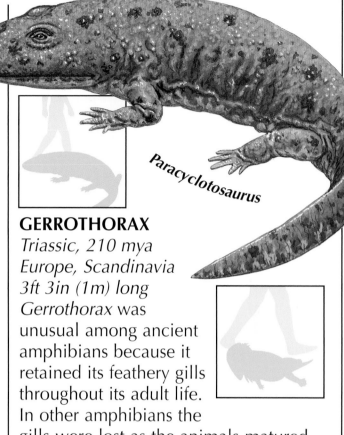

Paracyclotosaurus

GERROTHORAX

Triassic, 210 mya
Europe, Scandinavia
3ft 3in (1m) long
Gerrothorax was unusual among ancient amphibians because it retained its feathery gills throughout its adult life. In other amphibians the gills were lost as the animals matured from the larval stage (tadpoles) to their adult stage. *Gerrothorax*, which looked like a big tadpole with a flattened body, was able to breathe under water using its gills. It had a wide head, on the top of which were its eyes, set close together. It may have rested on the bed of a lake or a river, looking up through the water for a passing fish – and when one came close enough it ambushed it.

Gerrothorax

AMPHIBIAN LIFE CYCLE

Early amphibians, like today's toads and newts, began life in water. Larvae, called tadpoles, hatched from soft, jelly-covered eggs. They had gills. Front legs grew, then back legs. Adults lost their gills and breathed with lungs – on land and in water.

19

Acanthostega was an early tetrapod – an animal with four limbs which had fingers and toes. When the fossilized remains of this amphibian were first discovered it was thought to prove that animals had evolved legs in order to free them from a life in water – having legs meant they could move up on to the land. However, when the limbs of *Acanthostega* were looked at closely, it was realized that here was an animal that was much more at home in water than on the land.

FISH-LIKE TETRAPOD

Acanthostega had a mixture of fish-like and tetrapod features. It had the tail fin, nares (nostrils) and gills of a fish, and the legs and feet of a tetrapod.

HAPPIEST IN THE WATER

The limbs of *Acanthostega* are a clue to how it lived. Since its limbs lacked wrist and ankle joints, it is thought they would have been too weak to support its body weight out of water. So, perhaps *Acanthostega* spent most of its life in water, moving about by using its limbs as paddles. In shallow water it might also have been able to use its limbs to push its way through dense growths of plants. It had scales on its belly, but not on the rest of its body which, as in amphibians, was smooth. The scales suggest it needed to protect its soft underside, perhaps when it dragged itself on to dry land.

A group of Acanthostega *in the shallows of a lake. Some hunt for fish, others haul themselves on to land to grab at insects. A patch of spawn floats in the water. A predatory fish closes in on the group.*

ACANTHOSTEGA LIMBS

Acanthostega *had long limbs that ended in eight digits – its fingers and toes. Its feet were webbed, just like the feet of ducks and geese today. This would have helped Acanthostega to power through the water.*

ACANTHOSTEGA FACT FILE

Name: Acanthostega
Lived: 370 million years ago
Found: Greenland

Length: 2ft (60cm)
Diet: Fish, insects
Habitat: Lakes and ponds

VARIED DIET

The teeth of *Acanthostega* show that they were suited to catching fish, and other small water-living animals. It may also have caught small prey on land.

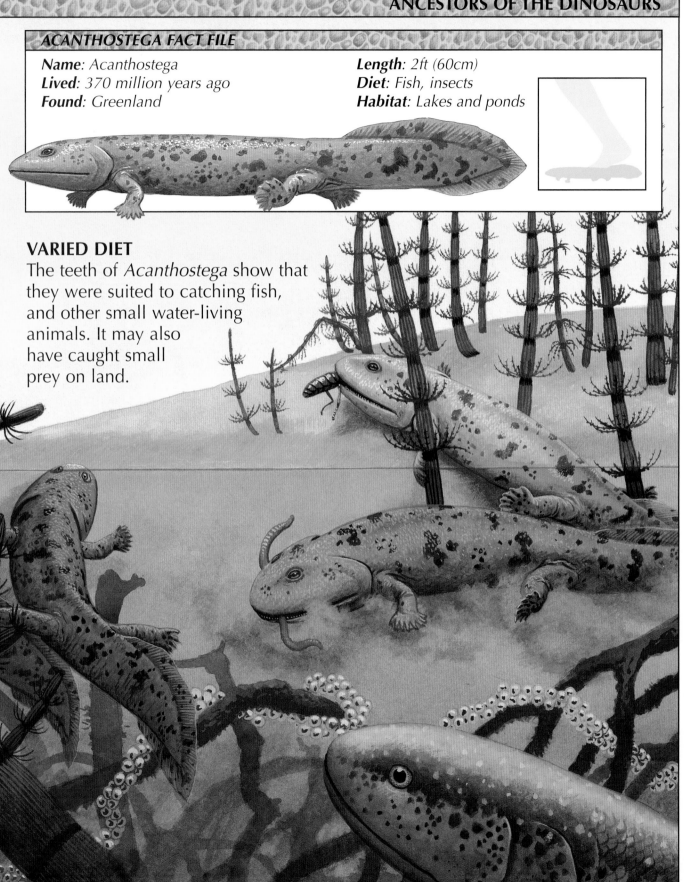

The first reptiles appeared between 350 and 300 million years ago. While the paddle-like limbs of their amphibian ancestors had been steadily evolving into arms and feet with fingers and toes, an even greater change had been happening at the same time – the development of eggs with hard shells. It was this step forward that gave reptiles the final freedom from water – they no longer had to return there to lay their eggs. They were free to colonize dry land.

However, some experts think that *Westlothiana* is not a true reptile at all. They say it is still more like an amphibian. For this reason it is known as a "reptiliomorph" – a form of reptile from which true reptiles evolved.

PETROLACOSAURUS

Carboniferous, 300 million years ago
North America
1ft 4in (40cm) long
An elegant, slender lizard, *Petrolacosaurus* is one of the oldest known diapsid reptiles. The diapsids were a group of reptiles characterized by two openings on the side of their skulls, to which groups of muscles were attached. The openings were located just behind the eyes. It was from early diapsids, such as *Petrolacosaurus*, that dinosaurs were later to evolve. Based on its resemblance to modern lizards, *Petrolacosaurus* was probably a fast-moving animal that chased after insects.

Westlothiana

WESTLOTHIANA

Carboniferous, 350 million years ago
Europe
1ft (30cm) long
Discovered in 1988, and named after the Westlothian district of Scotland where it was found, *Westlothiana lizziae* (or "Lizzie" for short) had a mixture of early tetrapod and early reptile features. *Westlothiana* lived close to a large freshwater lake, probably hunting for millipedes, harvestman spiders, and insects. It could be one of the oldest reptiles found.

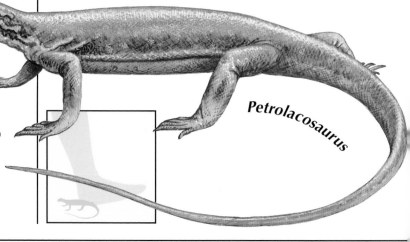

Petrolacosaurus

REPTILE EGGS

One of the most important characteristics of reptiles – ancient and modern – is that they lay hard-shelled eggs, known as amniotic eggs. Their hard shells mean that the contents of the egg do not dry out. For this reason they can be laid on dry land. The evolution of amniotic eggs made it possible for animals to live and breed on dry land, rather than having to return to water to lay their eggs, as amphibians do.

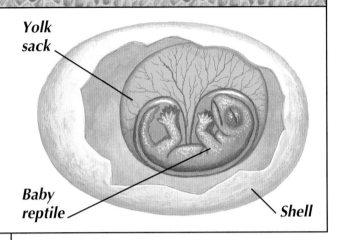

Yolk sack

Baby reptile

Shell

PALEOTHYRIS

Carboniferous, 300 mya
North America
1ft (30cm) long

A small, agile lizard-like creature, *Paleothyris* had sharp teeth and large eyes. It probably fed on insects and other small invertebrates (animals without backbones) which it chased after on the floor of its forest home. *Paleothyris* was an early reptile, yet it still had some features that were more amphibian-like than reptile-like, especially its skull. Dinosaurs were ultimately descended from creatures like *Paleothyris*, even though it was not yet a true reptile.

PAREIASAURUS

Permian, 250 million years ago
South Africa, Europe
8ft (2.5m) long

A heavily-built animal whose skin was covered with numerous interlocking bony scales, *Pareiasaurus* was a plant-eating reptile. The scales may have provided some protection against predators, as well as helping to stiffen its bulky body. Because *Pareiasaurus* was a relative of the turtles, it has been suggested that its scales might have evolved into their hard shells.

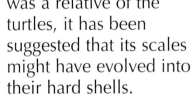

Pareiasaurus

In the long history of life on Earth, some kinds of animals failed to evolve beyond a certain stage – they were nature's dead ends. *Askeptosaurus* and the rest of its family of crocodile-like creatures fall into this category. Others, though, continued to develop, refining the features which made them successful. *Lagosuchus*, though not a dinosaur, had some features in common with them.

Scutosaurus

MILLERETTA

Permian, 250 million years ago
South Africa
2ft (60cm) long

Milleretta was a small, fast-moving early reptile that might have lived entirely on a diet of insects. Toward the back of its skull was a concave area which seems to suggest it had ear drums. If it did, then it probably had quite a good sense of hearing. Despite this advanced feature, *Milleretta* belongs to the anapsid group of reptiles, whose skulls are more like those of turtles, not lizards and snakes. This means that even though *Milleretta* was one of the first reptiles, it was not directly related to dinosaurs.

Milleretta

SCUTOSAURUS

Permian, 250 mya
Europe
8ft (2.5m) long

Similar in appearance to *Pareiasaurus*, to which it was related, *Scutosaurus* lived in small herds. It was a slow-moving bulky herbivore, feeding on vegetation that floated on the surfaces of freshwater lakes and pools. Its flat, leaf-shaped teeth had serrated edges which could easily cut through leaves and stems. There were gaps between its teeth, so water could freely drain from its mouth, leaving only the plants behind to be chewed. A fully-grown adult *Scutosaurus* grew a horn on its nose, and spikes pointed down from the jaw. Its skin was covered with bony projections – perhaps to protect it from meat-eating predators.

ASKEPTOSAURUS
Triassic, 220 mya
Europe
6ft 6in (2m) long
Askeptosaurus belonged to a family of early diapsid reptiles known as thalattosaurs. They were crocodile-like animals that seem to have spent most of their time in the water, only venturing on to land in order to lay their eggs. *Askeptosaurus* was a slender animal, with a long neck, body and tail. As a swimmer it probably moved like an eel, snaking its way quickly through the water. It was a fish-eater and might have been able to dive quite deep in search of its prey, which it snapped up with its long, toothy jaws.

Lagosuchus

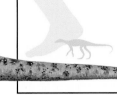

LAGOSUCHUS
Triassic, 230 mya
South America
1ft 4in (40cm) long
A lightly-built early reptile, *Lagosuchus* is notable for its long, slender legs and well-developed feet – features it shares with many kinds of dinosaurs. With a body like this, *Lagosuchus* was made for running. Perhaps it used its ability to run fast to chase after insects which it caught and ate. It would also have put its speed to use when escaping from a predator who might have been out to catch it.

Askeptosaurus

REPTILE HANDS

The shape of an animal's hands reveals a lot about its lifestyle. Amphibians' hands are not good for grasping. Instead, with their webbed fingers and toes they are better suited to paddling through water. A reptile's hand is much more advanced, with long slender fingers that can grasp and pull at things, and dig into the ground.

Amphibian hand

Reptile hand

The story of life on Earth is the story of evolution – how living things have learned to adapt to changes over time. Some of the adaptations evolved by the early reptiles became important features of dinosaurs, pterosaurs and plesiosaurs. The diapsid skull, present in some early reptiles, is one such example, as is the ability to stand on two legs – a feature seen in *Euparkeria* and which became fully evolved in the meat-eating dinosaurs that came later. Other features, such as the strange scales of *Longisquama*, were not passed on to the dinosaurs.

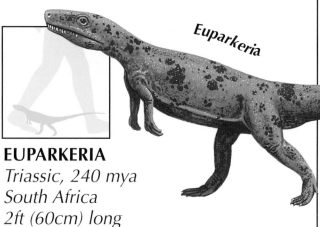

Euparkeria

EUPARKERIA
Triassic, 240 mya
South Africa
2ft (60cm) long
A lightly-built meat-eating animal, *Euparkeria* had longer hind limbs than forelimbs, making it unlike most other early reptiles of its time. This distinctive feature may well have meant that *Euparkeria* could rear up on its hind limbs and run on two legs over short distances – one of the first reptiles to have this ability. Being able to run on two legs would have given *Euparkeria* an advantage over slower four-footed reptiles. It was from reptiles such as *Euparkeria* that dinosaurs and pterosaurs evolved.

LONGISQUAMA
Triassic, 230 million years ago
Asia
6in (15cm) long
This strange-looking creature is named after the unusual scales that grew in two rows along its back. These long, curved, bony projections have puzzled scientists since the reptile was first discovered in 1969. If these scales were held straight out on either side of its body, then perhaps *Longisquama* could have used them as an airfoil, giving it a "wingspan" of about 1ft (30cm). If this is so, then it might have been able to glide through forests.

Not everyone agrees with this. Some scientists think the scales were brightly colored, and were used in courtship displays.

Longisquama

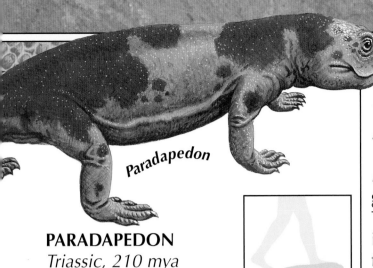

Paradapedon

HYPSOGNATHUS

Triassic, 210 million years ago
North America
1ft 1in (33cm) long
Hypsognathus had bony spikes growing from the sides of its head. They were probably used to defend it if it was attacked. By flicking its head from side to side the spikes would have forced a predator to keep its distance. It was a herbivore, and it chewed on plants with blunt, peg-like teeth which were at the back of its mouth. A small, squat animal, Hypsognathus was probably a slow-mover.

PARADAPEDON

Triassic, 210 mya
Asia
4ft (1.3m) long
Paradapedon was a rhynchosaur – a barrel-shaped, pig-like animal that walked on all-fours. Rhynchosaurs were the most abundant reptiles of the mid to late Triassic period (about 220–200 million years ago). Like other rhynchosaurs, Paradapedon was a plant-eater. It used its beak to bite through tough plants, such as seed ferns. When conifers replaced ferns in the Jurassic period, the rhynchosaurs died out.

Hypsognathus

HOLES IN THE HEAD

Reptiles are divided into groups based on the number of holes in their skulls, to which muscles are attached:
1. Anapsids: have no holes.
2. Synapsids: have one hole either side.

3. Diapsids: have two holes either side. Dinosaurs, pterosaurs, and plesiosaurs evolved from the diapsid reptiles. Diapsids alive today include crocodiles, lizards, snakes and birds.

Skull openings

1. Anapsid
2. Synapsid
3. Diapsid

1   2   3

Eye socket

Nostril

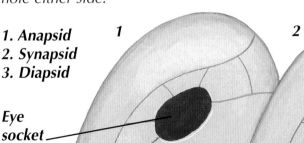

HYLONOMUS

One of the very first reptiles known to have lived on Earth was found at a famous fossil site at Joggins, in Nova Scotia, Canada. Here, sea action is constantly eroding the cliffs to reveal evidence of ancient animal and plant life. It was in 1851 that the fossilized remains of a new kind of prehistoric animal were discovered at the Joggins fossil site. It was given the name *Hylonomus*, which means "forest mouse." A small reptile, it lived about 310 million years ago.

LIZARD-LIKE

Hylonomus was one of the anapsid reptiles – the first group of primitive reptiles to evolve. As an anapsid its skull was solid – it was still like that of an amphibian. The only holes in its skull were for its eyes and nostrils. It probably did not have an ear drum. *Hylonomus* looked like a small lizard, and it probably lived like one too. It had a long, slender body and tail, four well-developed limbs, and its jaws were packed with small, sharp teeth.

Hylonomus *reptiles on the floor of their forest home, shortly after a flood has felled many of the trees. One* Hylonomus *is about to climb into a rotten tree stump, from which it will be unable to climb back out.*

HYLONOMUS FACT FILE

Name: *Hylonomus*
Lived: *310 million years ago*
Found: *Canada*

Length: *8in (20cm)*
Diet: *Spiders, millipedes, insects*
Habitat: *Forest floors*

FOREST FLOOR

Hylonomus lived on the floor of a forest in which trees grew to 100ft (30m). Seed ferns grew on the ground. In this shaded habitat, *Hylonomus* hid from predators, searched for food, and raised its young.

SHARP TEETH

A meat-eater, *Hylonomus* probably lived on a diet of insects and other small invertebrates, such as millipedes, worms, and spiders. Its sharp, pointed teeth would have bitten through these soft-bodied animals with ease. Its teeth may also have been able to puncture the hard shells of land snails, before its jaws closed and crushed the snails to pieces.

TRAPPED INSIDE TREE STUMPS

We know about Hylonomus *because several complete fossils have been found, all in one place. Millions of years ago a forest of scaly barked trees was flooded. The trees fell. After the flood,* Hylonomus *reptiles crept into the rotting tree stumps in search of insects. They became trapped, and died.*

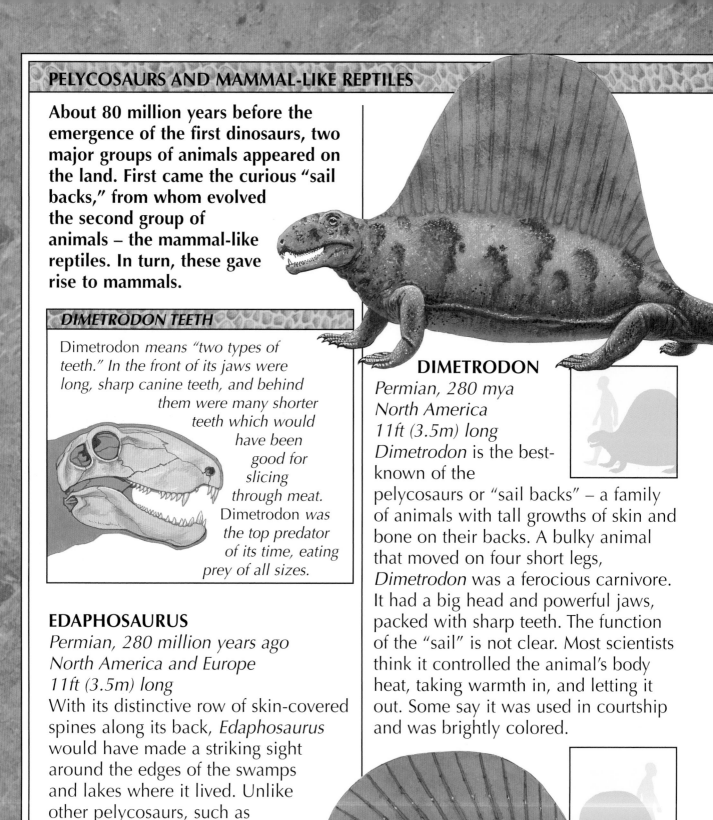

About 80 million years before the emergence of the first dinosaurs, two major groups of animals appeared on the land. First came the curious "sail backs," from whom evolved the second group of animals – the mammal-like reptiles. In turn, these gave rise to mammals.

DIMETRODON TEETH

Dimetrodon *means "two types of teeth." In the front of its jaws were long, sharp canine teeth, and behind them were many shorter teeth which would have been good for slicing through meat.* Dimetrodon *was the top predator of its time, eating prey of all sizes.*

DIMETRODON
Permian, 280 mya
North America
11ft (3.5m) long
Dimetrodon is the best-known of the pelycosaurs or "sail backs" – a family of animals with tall growths of skin and bone on their backs. A bulky animal that moved on four short legs, *Dimetrodon* was a ferocious carnivore. It had a big head and powerful jaws, packed with sharp teeth. The function of the "sail" is not clear. Most scientists think it controlled the animal's body heat, taking warmth in, and letting it out. Some say it was used in courtship and was brightly colored.

EDAPHOSAURUS
Permian, 280 million years ago
North America and Europe
11ft (3.5m) long
With its distinctive row of skin-covered spines along its back, *Edaphosaurus* would have made a striking sight around the edges of the swamps and lakes where it lived. Unlike other pelycosaurs, such as *Dimetrodon, Edaphosaurus* was a herbivore. Its teeth were blunt and peg-like, which suggests they were used for chopping and chewing on plants, not on meat.

TITANOSUCHUS

Permian, 270 mya
South Africa
8ft (2.5m) long
Titanosuchus belonged to a group of mammal-like reptiles (or reptile-like mammals) known as therapsids. These animals are the direct ancestors of the mammals, who began to appear around 200 million years ago. Therapsids had features which belonged to both reptiles and mammals. *Titanosuchus* was a predator. It had sharp incisor teeth and fang-like canines, perfect for biting and stabbing at prey, such as *Moschops*, a large, slow-moving plant-eater.

Titanosuchus

MOSCHOPS

Permian, 260 mya
South Africa
16ft (5m) long
The biggest of all the mammal-like reptiles was *Moschops*, a herbivore with a barrel-shaped body, short tail, and thick legs. Inside its bulky body was a massive gut – a typical feature of most plant-eating animals. *Moschops* needed a long gut to process the vegetation it ate, extracting the maximum amount of energy from its food. Like other herbivores it had blunt teeth. From the fossils found, it seems that *Moschops* lived in small herds, grazing on low-lying plants, just as cattle do today.

Moschops

31

The mammal-like reptiles – therapsids – were a major group of ancient animals. They appeared about 300 million years ago, and survived for 120 million years. Their skulls were like those of mammals, but most of them walked like reptiles.

ESTEMMENOSUCHUS
Permian, 255 mya
Europe
10ft (3m) long

Estemmenosuchus

TAPINOCEPHALUS
Permian, 270 million years ago
South Africa
13ft (4m) long

A large and strongly built mammal-like reptile, *Tapinocephalus* was a slow-moving herbivore, similar to *Moschops* which lived in the same region and at the same time. Like others in its family, *Tapinocephalus* had an unusually thick skull. No one knows for certain why this was – some scientists think it shows that *Tapinocephalus* was a head-butting animal. Perhaps adults clashed their heads together to decide who was the strongest member of a group.

A huge mammal-like reptile, *Estemmenosuchus* lived on the edges of pools and lakes, perhaps in herds. It might have had a diet of plants, such as horsetails, and small animals. A mixed diet like this would make it an omnivore. Its most striking feature was a "crown" of bony horns. Their function is not known. They may have been used in courtship displays, when rival adults locked horns, as stags do today.

Tapinocephalus

ROBERTIA

Permian, 260 million years ago
South Africa
8in (20cm) long

Robertia belongs to a family of mammal-like reptiles known as the dicynodonts ("two dog teeth"). They are named after their two canine teeth which looked like small tusks – the only teeth they had. These long teeth grew down from the upper jaw. *Robertia*, like other dicynodonts, was a pig-like herbivore, able to tug at and bite through vegetation with its beak. One of the first dicynodonts to appear, it is thought that *Robertia* might have lived in a burrow – safely out of sight of any predators that might have hunted it.

Robertia

PROCYNOSUCHUS

Permian, 260 million years ago
South Africa, Europe
2ft (60cm) long

Procynosuchus was a cynodont – a member of the "dog-toothed" group of mammal-like reptiles. It was not a typical cynodont, since *Procynosuchus* had become adapted to life in water – cynodonts were more usually to be found living on the land. It swam by wiggling the front and rear ends of its stiff spine, like a crocodile, and paddled with its otter-like webbed hands and feet. *Procynosuchus* was a meat-eater.

HORNED HEAD

Estemmenosuchus, which means "crowned crocodile," is named after the "crown" of horns that grew on its skull. They could have been used in fights. They would also have shielded its eyes from harm. An adult's skull was 18in (45cm) wide – the size of a rhinoceros skull.

Procynosuchus

Among the later mammal-like reptiles were ones that had evolved true features of mammals. There was *Thrinaxodon*, which might have been hairy, and *Lycaenops*, a long-legged animal that walked with an upright posture, not a sprawling one like reptiles.

CISTECEPHALUS

Permian, 260 million years ago
South Africa
1ft 1in (33cm) long

Cistecephalus

Cistecephalus lived in underground tunnels, as moles and molerats do today. A small, strongly-built animal, *Cistecephalus* would have dug into the ground with its front paws, scratching away at the soil which it kicked out of the way with its back feet. In its dark, subterranean world, this mammal-like reptile would have eaten worms, beetles, snails and other small animals which fell into its tunnel network. *Cistecephalus* may also have eaten the soft underground stems of horsetails and ferns.

LYCAENOPS

Lycaenops

Permian, 260 mya
South Africa
3ft 3in (1m) long
Lycaenops – its name means "wolf face" – was a lightly built meat-eater with long legs. Like the wolf of today, *Lycaenops* had a long and slender skull, with very long dog-like canine teeth set into both its upper and lower jaws. Pointed canine teeth were ideal for stabbing and tearing at the flesh of large prey, such as the herbivore *Moschops*, which it may have hunted. *Lycaenops* may have been a pack animal, living and hunting with others of its kind.

WALKING TALL

Lycaenops *walked and ran with its long legs held close to its body. This is a feature found in mammals, but not in reptiles whose legs are positioned to the sides of their bodies. The ability to move like a mammal would have given* Lycaenops *an advantage over other four-legged animals, since it would have been able to out-run them.*

THRINAXODON

Triassic, 250 mya
South Africa, Antarctica
1ft 8in (50cm) long

Thrinaxodon

LYSTROSAURUS

Triassic, 250 million years ago
South Africa, Asia, Antarctica
3ft 3in (1m) long

Lystrosaurus was a herbivore. It was a mammal-like reptile that belonged to the dicynodont group of animals – those with two canine teeth growing from their upper jaw. Its snout ended in a bony beak, like that of a tortoise, and would have been used to pull at and cut through vegetation. It is thought to have lived on the margins of lakes, and, like a modern hippopotamus, it might have spent time in the water feeding on aquatic plants.

Thrinaxodon was a small meat-eating cynodont – an animal characterized by having dog-like canine, molar and incisor teeth. *Thrinaxodon* was able to breathe while eating, an ability that mammals have but reptiles do not. It is suspected that *Thrinaxodon* was covered in hair – another important mammal-like feature not present in reptiles. Despite its looks, *Thrinaxodon*'s skeleton still had reptile-like features, which is why it is classed as a mammal-like reptile. It lived in burrows, coming out to hunt for its prey.

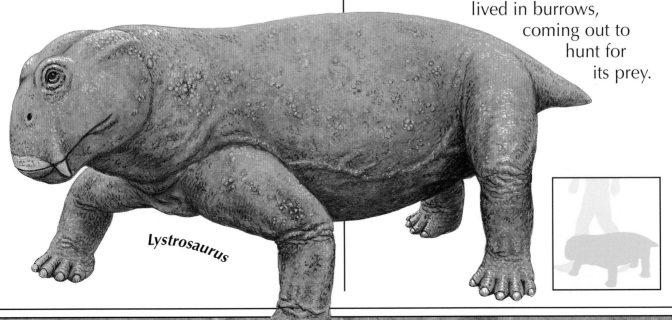

Lystrosaurus

THE PERMIAN MASS EXTINCTION

Toward the end of the Permian period of Earth's history, about 248 million years ago, something happened that led to the death of almost all life on the planet. It was the largest mass extinction of animal species ever to happen – greater even than that which wiped out the dinosaurs millions of years later.

The Permian mass extinction event killed off an estimated 70 per cent of all life on the land, and 90 per cent of all life in the sea. It might have taken as little as 100,000 years for Earth's animal life to die out – some scientists say it happened in only 10,000 years! The cause – or causes – are not certain: many theories exist to explain what happened so long ago.

DEATH FROM VOLCANOES

Massive volcanic eruptions in Siberia, Northern Eurasia, happened at the end of the Permian period. They would have sent huge amounts of carbon dioxide and other gases into the atmosphere, causing acid rain to fall. This would have killed plant life. Animals could have starved.

DEATH BY SUFFOCATION

An increase in carbon dioxide in the atmosphere, from volcanic eruptions, would reduce the amount of oxygen in air and water. For animals everywhere this would have been a death sentence, and they would have suffocated.

As vegetation died out, the plant-eaters would have died with it. Meat-eaters would have become more and more desperate to find dwindling supplies of food.

DEATH FROM SPACE

A theory gaining support from scientists is that Earth was hit by a meteorite – a space rock. There is good evidence that the dinosaurs were wiped out when a meteorite struck the Earth 65 million years ago, so maybe a space rock also destroyed life on Earth 248 million years ago. If the impact was big enough it could have set off volcanic eruptions, and filled the atmosphere with deadly gases.

DEATH BY FREEZING

Another idea is that the Earth's temperature dropped, which led to the expansion of polar ice from the North and South poles. Evidence has been found for a cooling of the climate towards the end of the Permian period, but whether it was cold enough – or the drop in temperature lasted long enough – to kill off the world's animal life is not at all clear.

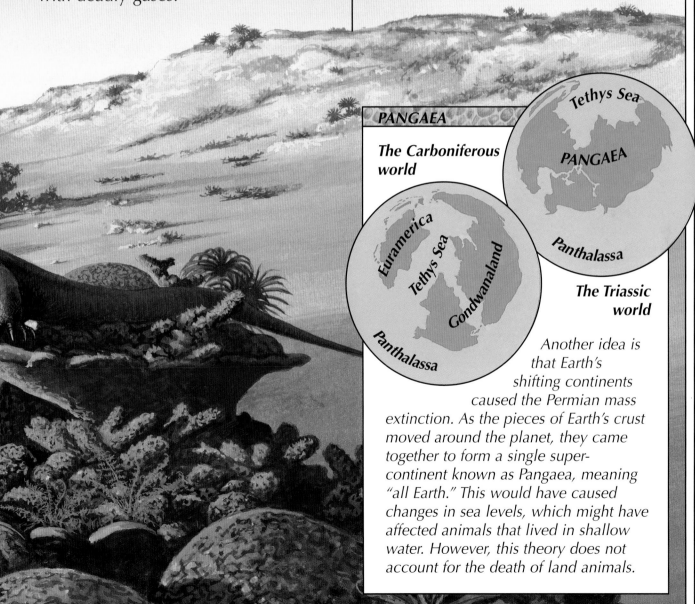

PANGAEA

The Carboniferous world

Euramerica
Tethys Sea
Gondwanaland
Panthalassa

Tethys Sea
PANGAEA
Panthalassa

The Triassic world

Another idea is that Earth's shifting continents caused the Permian mass extinction. As the pieces of Earth's crust moved around the planet, they came together to form a single super-continent known as Pangaea, meaning "all Earth." This would have caused changes in sea levels, which might have affected animals that lived in shallow water. However, this theory does not account for the death of land animals.

The catastrophe that wiped out most of Earth's animal life at the end of the Permian period, about 248 million years ago, changed the course of evolution. From the survivors came animals such as *Cynognathus* – still a mammal-like reptile, but with features more like those of mammals than reptiles. However, before mammals came to dominate the world, the dinosaurs ruled.

CYNOGNATHUS

Triassic, 230 million years ago
South Africa, South America,
Antarctica
3ft 3in (1m) long
Cynognathus was a predator that hunted in packs for prey such as *Kannemeyeria*. Unlike other mammal-like reptiles, it had an upright posture, not a sprawling one. It might have been hair-covered, and its young might have been born live, not from eggs.

KANNEMEYERIA

Triassic, 230 mya
South Africa,
Asia,
South
America,
Antarctica
10ft (3m) long
A massive herbivore with sprawling legs, *Kannemeyeria* was a mammal-like reptile of the dicynodont family – animals with two canine teeth growing from their upper jaws. These were its only teeth, and its snout ended in a bony beak. *Kannemeyeria* lived in an open landscape, where it was hunted by predators such as *Cynognathus.*

Cynognathus

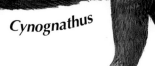

TEETH LIKE A MAMMAL'S

Cynognathus, *which means "dog jaw," was a cynodont – an animal with dog-like teeth. It had powerful jaws packed with sharp incisors at the front, fang-like canines behind them, and cheek teeth edged with saw-like points – ideal for shearing through meat. Teeth like these show that* Cynognathus *was closely related to mammals.*

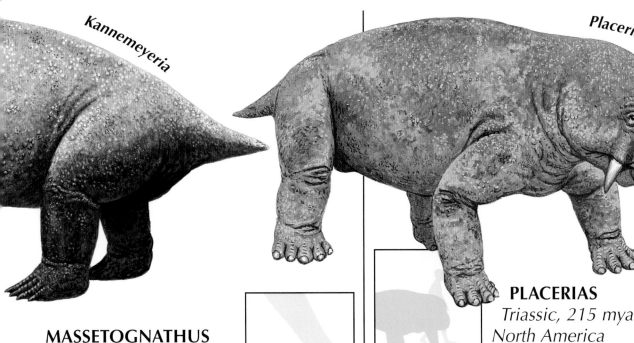

Kannemeyeria

Placerias

MASSETOGNATHUS
Triassic, 220 mya
South America
1ft 8in (50cm) long
Not all cynodonts were meat-eaters.
The medium-sized *Massetognathus* was
a plant-eater with cheek teeth specially
adapted to chewing on vegetation. It
still had the distinctive long snout of
the cynodont family, with nipping
incisors and fang-like canines, but its
cheek teeth were not pointed. Instead
they were flat-topped and were
covered with a number of low ridges,
which made them good for grinding
away at stems, roots and other plant
material. *Massetognathus* had clawed
feet and a long dog-like tail. It may
have been covered with hair.

Massetognathus

PLACERIAS
Triassic, 215 mya
North America
11ft (3.5m) long
The two tusks in the upper jaw of
Placerias show that it was a member of
the dicynodont family of mammal-like
reptiles. In front of its tusks was a large,
bony beak. In a fully-grown adult the
skull was about 2ft (60cm) long.
Placerias was a herbivore. It probably
used its tusks to dig into the ground,
uprooting vegetation to eat. Its beak
was used to shear through plant
material – from tough roots to soft
stems and leaves. *Placerias* looked a
little like a hippopotamus – it was
bulky, had short legs, and wide,
spreading feet with blunt claws. It
might have lived in a seasonal
environment, in which there were two
seasons each year, one dry, the other
wet. *Placerias* probably lived in herds,
close to water. It was one of the last of
the dicynodonts, which, for some
reason, became extinct about
210 million years ago.

CHAPTER TWO

KILLERS AND SCAVENGERS

THEROPODS – THE MEAT-EATERS

In 1881, Othniel Charles Marsh (1831–99), a famous American fossil-hunter, said that all meat-eating dinosaurs (the carnivores) should be grouped together. Marsh suggested a name for this group. He said they should be called theropods, meaning "beast feet." The first theropods appeared about 225 million years ago, not long after the Mesozoic Era – the Age of Reptiles – had begun. Meat-eating dinosaurs survived for 160 million years, right until the time that dinosaurs died out, 65 million years ago.

CREATURE FEATURES

Most meat-eating dinosaurs walked on two slender legs that ended in three-toed, bird-like feet with sharp claws. They were able to move quite fast – certainly faster than the slower-moving plant-eating dinosaurs. Their arms were short, their chests were compact, their tails were long, their necks were curved and flexible, and their eyes were big.

CHANGES OVER TIME

The meat-eaters evolved over the course of their 160-million-year existence. Their brains became larger, their limbs longer and more slender, and their eyesight improved.

Daspletosaurus

Albertosaurus

Dromaeosaurus

Meat-eating dinosaurs lived on Earth for about 160 million years. There were many different species. They were the top predators of the Mesozoic Era.

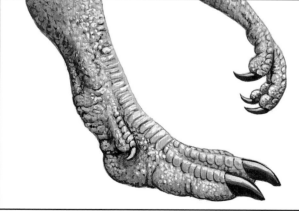

Hand and foot of a meat-eating dinosaur.

TEETH AND BEAKS

Carnivorous dinosaurs either had teeth or beaks. Theropod teeth were thin and blade-like, with serrated ridges that ran along their front and back edges. When the carnivore bit into its prey, the serrations hooked themselves into the victim's flesh, cutting like the teeth on a saw blade deep into the meat. Small-sized meat-eaters generally had more teeth packed into their jaws than larger carnivores did. In toothed meat-eaters the longest teeth were to be found in the middle of their jaws, where more biting power could be applied by the jaw muscles. Some meat-eaters evolved jaws that had no teeth in them at all. Instead, these toothless theropods had bony beaks covered by a layer of horn. Unsuitable for biting into meat, their beaks might have been used for cracking open eggs.

Dromiceiomimus

Trodon

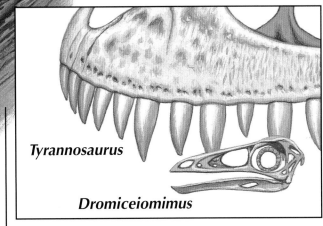

Tyrannosaurus

Dromiceiomimus

Some meat-eaters had teeth, some had beaks.

THE FIRST MEAT-EATERS

The first meat-eating dinosaurs appeared during the middle of the Triassic period, about 225 million years ago. They were quite a lot smaller, and not as highly evolved, as the better known larger carnivores that came later in the Mesozoic, such as **Tyrannosaurus rex**.

EORAPTOR

Triassic, 225 mya
South America
3ft 3in (1m) long

Eoraptor is an important animal because it is one of the world's oldest known dinosaurs – it lived near the very beginning of the Age of Reptiles. *Eoraptor* was a small dinosaur that moved around quickly on two long, slender legs. Its legs were twice as long as its arms. It was a meat-eater, and it may have been both a hunter and a scavenger. Inside its long jaws were many small, serrated teeth. *Eoraptor* fossils have been unearthed along the course of an ancient river in Argentina. This has led scientists to wonder if *Eoraptor* was a fish-eater.

Eoraptor

COELOPHYSIS

Triassic, 220 mya
North America
10ft (3m) long

Coelophysis

Coelophysis was built for pace and agility. To keep its weight down, its leg bones were almost hollow – a great help to an animal that relied on speed to catch its prey. Its front legs were small and were probably used for clawing and grasping at food. It might have been a pack animal, living and hunting in groups.

FAST MOVERS

Speed and agility were two crucially important abilities that meat-eating dinosaurs had to have. Without these skills, their chances of survival would have been reduced. Meat-eaters had to be capable of running as fast as the prey they lived off.

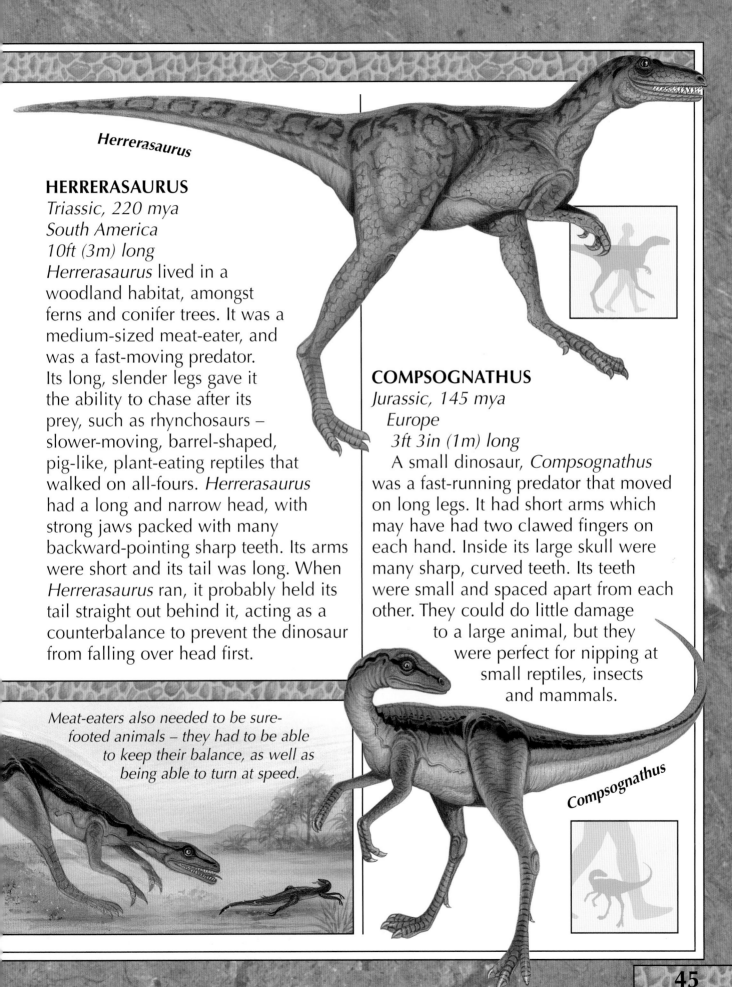

Herrerasaurus

HERRERASAURUS

Triassic, 220 mya
South America
10ft (3m) long
Herrerasaurus lived in a woodland habitat, amongst ferns and conifer trees. It was a medium-sized meat-eater, and was a fast-moving predator. Its long, slender legs gave it the ability to chase after its prey, such as rhynchosaurs – slower-moving, barrel-shaped, pig-like, plant-eating reptiles that walked on all-fours. *Herrerasaurus* had a long and narrow head, with strong jaws packed with many backward-pointing sharp teeth. Its arms were short and its tail was long. When *Herrerasaurus* ran, it probably held its tail straight out behind it, acting as a counterbalance to prevent the dinosaur from falling over head first.

Meat-eaters also needed to be sure-footed animals – they had to be able to keep their balance, as well as being able to turn at speed.

COMPSOGNATHUS

Jurassic, 145 mya
Europe
3ft 3in (1m) long
A small dinosaur, *Compsognathus* was a fast-running predator that moved on long legs. It had short arms which may have had two clawed fingers on each hand. Inside its large skull were many sharp, curved teeth. Its teeth were small and spaced apart from each other. They could do little damage to a large animal, but they were perfect for nipping at small reptiles, insects and mammals.

Compsognathus

45

Large-sized meat-eaters began to appear in the Jurassic period. They reached their greatest size in the following time zone, the Cretaceous. Powerfully-built, and equipped with sharp meat-slicing teeth and claws that could scratch and rip into the thickest skin, these theropods might have roamed the land in small groups, as well as in ones and twos.

DILOPHOSAURUS

Jurassic, 190 million years ago
North America
20ft (6m) long
One of the earliest large-sized meat-eaters, *Dilophosaurus* is notable because of the unusual double crests of bone that grew on top of its head. It is not clear what they were for, or whether they appeared on both males and females.

One idea is that the crests were brightly colored, and could have been used as signaling devices, perhaps to attract a mate at breeding time, or to mark an individual out as the leader of a group. Long claws grew from the toes of *Dilophosaurus*. They might have been used as weapons when it attacked another animal, kicking at it while its hands grasped at it. Scientists think that *Dilophosaurus* was a group animal that lived in small herds.

ALLOSAURUS

Jurassic/Cretaceous,
140 mya
North America
40ft (12m) long
Allosaurus was the largest meat-eater of the early Cretaceous period. It walked on two powerful legs and had a thick, S-shaped neck. Its arms were short, with hands that had three curved and pointed claws, each up to 6in (15cm) long. Inside its jaws were many backward-pointing teeth, serrated like steak knives so they could slice easily through meat. Each tooth was up to 4in (10cm) long. When attacking an animal larger than itself, *Allosaurus* may have hunted in packs. It probably hunted smaller prey on its own.

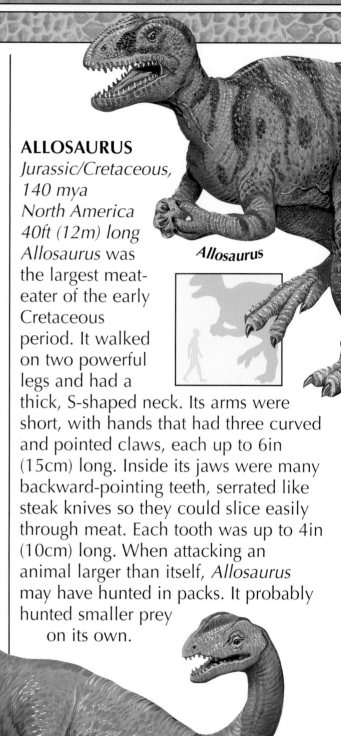

Allosaurus

Dilophosaurus

NEOVENATOR

Cretaceous, 125 mya
Europe
26ft (8m) long

Neovenator is related to the *Allosaurus* of North America, but it was more lightly-built. It was a fierce predator whose large skull contained razor-sharp teeth 2in (5cm) long. Claws up to 5in (13cm) long grew on its fingers. This array of weaponry marked out *Neovenator* as a formidable opponent in a fight, and with its long legs it would have been able to move about swiftly, probably breaking into a run over short distances. It has been found on the Isle of Wight, off the south coast of Britain, where it might have hunted the plant-eating *Iguanodon*.

Neovenator

SCAVENGERS

It is thought that meat-eating dinosaurs were scavengers as well as predators. While predators would have been active hunters, stalking their prey then killing it, scavengers ate meat from animals that had been killed by others. Scavenging for "free meals" saved energy, without the danger of getting hurt in a fight.

GIGANOTOSAURUS

Cretaceous, 90 mya
South America
49ft (15m) long

Giganotosaurus was a giant carnivore, 6ft (2m) longer than *Tyrannosaurus rex*. Because several were found together, it is thought it hunted in packs. It was probably also a lone predator. Its biggest teeth were 5in (20cm) long. They would have sliced deep into the flesh of a prey animal, inflicting wounds from which it died.

Giganotosaurus

These were some of the giants of the meat-eating dinosaurs – animals whose teeth, claws and muscular bodies were perfectly designed to attack their prey. Whether they acted alone or in packs, these theropods were among the most formidable of all hunters in the Age of Reptiles.

Ceratosaurus

CERATOSAURUS

Jurassic, 150 mya
North America,
Africa
20ft (6m) long
Ceratosaurus had a short horn on the tip of its snout, and horny ridges grew near its eyes. It is not thought these bumps were used as weapons. Instead, they might have been used for display purposes. *Ceratosaurus* had a large head. When it ate, the bones of its skull moved from side to side, allowing it to gulp down big pieces of meat. When its teeth fell out, because of old age, disease or damage, new ones grew to replace them.

MEGALOSAURUS

Jurassic, 170 mya
Europe
30ft (9m) long
Megalosaurus was the very first dinosaur to be named, in 1822. Despite this, little is known about it. No complete fossil skeletons have been found, so scientists have tried to work out its lifestyle from that of other meat-eaters. They believe it was a predatory dinosaur that hunted herbivores, such as *Iguanodon*. *Megalosaurus* might also have been a scavenger, eating flesh from an animal that was already dead. Like a lion, it may have stayed in the vicinity of a kill for several days, returning to feed on the carcass.

Megalosaurus

PACK HUNTERS

Hunting in packs gave meat-eaters the advantage over their prey. While one predator distracted the victim, forcing it to leave the safety of its herd, the pack closed in for the kill.

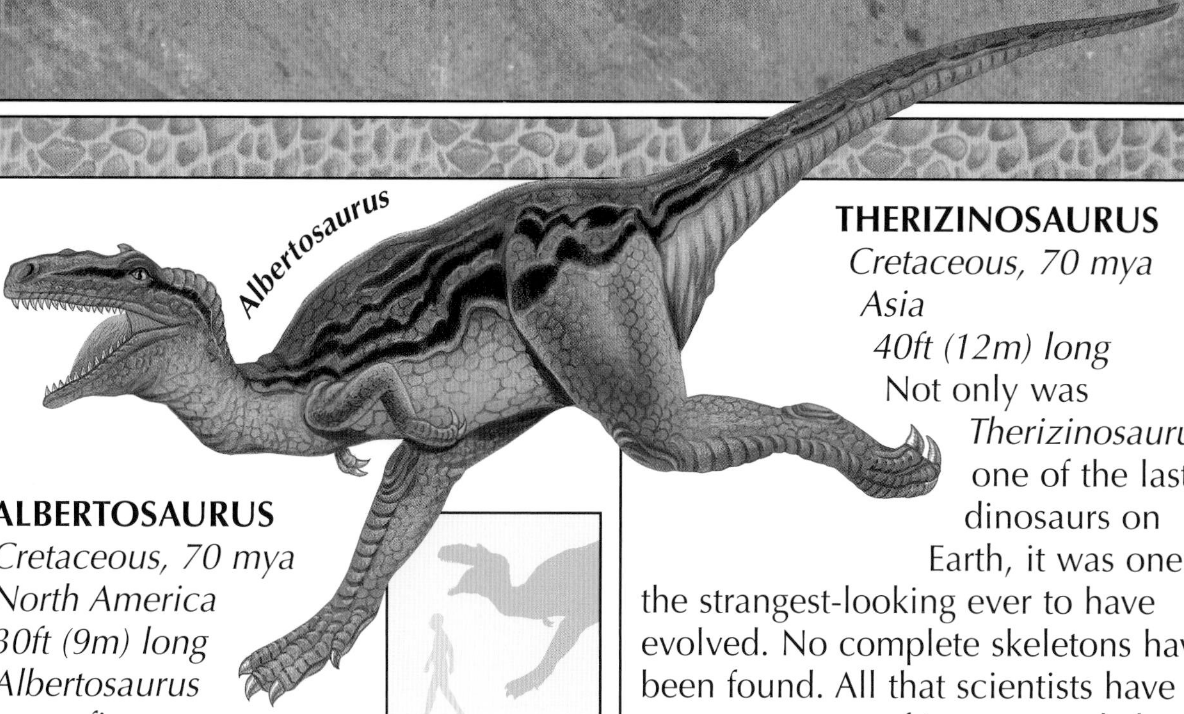

Albertosaurus

THERIZINOSAURUS
Cretaceous, 70 mya
Asia
40ft (12m) long
Not only was
Therizinosaurus
one of the last
dinosaurs on
Earth, it was one of
the strangest-looking ever to have
evolved. No complete skeletons have
been found. All that scientists have to
go on are parts of its arms and chest.
By comparing them with dinosaurs in
the same family, they think
Therizinosaurus might have looked like
the picture seen below, with a small
head at the end of a long neck. Its arms
were 8ft (2.45m) long, at the end of
which were three huge claws, the
longest of which grew to 2ft 4in
(70cm). Why it needed such long claws
puzzles scientists. Some believe
Therizinosaurus used its
giant claws to rip open
termite nests; others say
it used them to drag
plants towards its
mouth. Most agree it
was a meat-eater.

ALBERTOSAURUS
Cretaceous, 70 mya
North America
30ft (9m) long
Albertosaurus
was a fierce
predator and was a relative of
Tyrannosaurus. However, unlike
Tyrannosaurus, whose eyes looked
straight ahead, the eyes of
Albertosaurus were on the sides of its
head – so it might have had difficulty
seeing in front of it. To make up for its
poor eyesight it may have had a good
sense of smell. In front of its eyes were
two small horns which it may have
used for display purposes. It walked on
two strong muscular back legs, and
was probably a fast runner, with
a top speed over a short
distance of up to 20 mph (30 kph).

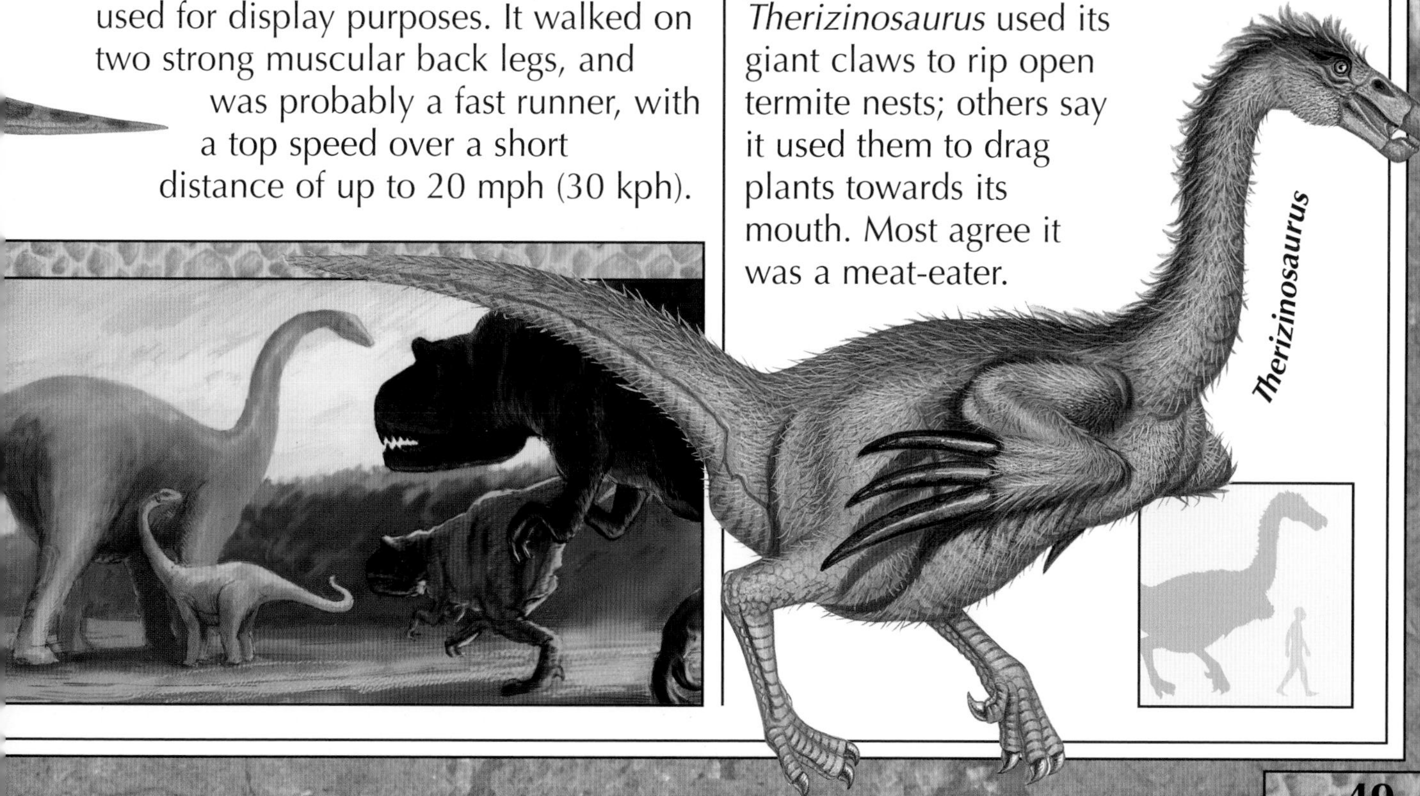

Therizinosaurus

TYRANNOSAURUS REX

Perhaps the best-known of all the dinosaurs, *Tyrannosaurus rex* only appeared shortly before they died out.

Name: Tyrannosaurus rex
Lived: 70 mya
Found: North America
Length: 40ft (12m)
Diet: Meat
Habitat: Open woodland

POWERFUL KILLER

Tyrannosaurus rex was one of the largest of all meat-eating predatory dinosaurs (*Giganotosaurus* was bigger). It was a strongly-built theropod that stood on two powerful legs, holding its back level with the ground, its tail outstretched for balance. Its forward-facing eyes probably gave it good vision, to help it hunt for prey.

SURPRISE ATTACKER

Tyrannosaurus rex lived in open woodland. It was a habitat in which there were clearings, and stands of conifers, cycads, oak, maple and beech trees, while on the ground were ferns and flowering plants. Grazing on the lush vegetation were plant-eaters, which *Tyrannosaurus rex* stalked. If at first it couldn't see them, perhaps it caught their scent – it seems that this dinosaur had a keen sense of smell. With a victim in sight, *Tyrannosaurus rex* charged it down at speeds of over 20 mph (36 kph), each of its giant strides covering 12 to 15ft (3.7–4.6m) of ground at a time.

BIG HEAD, BIG TEETH

Tyrannosaurus rex *had a massive head – about 5ft (1.5m) long. Its skull had large holes in it which helped to reduce its weight, making it light to carry around. Packed into its jaws were 50 to 60 blade-like teeth, some up to 9in (23cm) long.*

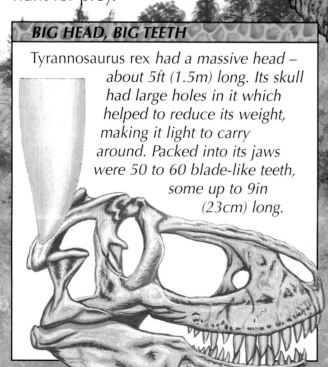

FULL TO BURSTING

Like a modern meat-eating animal such as a lion, *Tyrannosaurus rex* probably didn't eat every day. Instead, after it had killed its prey – a plant-eating animal – it gorged itself on the flesh, then ate nothing until it returned to the carcass for another meal a few days later. It may also have been a scavenger, feeding on animals killed by others.

An adult Tyrannosaurus rex *breaks cover and lunges at a plant-eating* Edmontosaurus *in a surprise attack.*

SMALL ARMS, HOOKED FINGERS

Tyrannosaurus rex *had short arms, with two clawed fingers on each hand. For such a strong animal its arms seem surprisingly feeble – but not if you imagine them used as hooks to hang on to its prey.*

Among the most recognizable of all the meat-eating dinosaurs were those with "sails" of skin on their backs. These were the spinosaurs – large, fish-eating theropods who had long, crocodile-like jaws, and finger claws shaped like sickles.

SUCHOMIMUS
Cretaceous, 105 mya
North Africa
36ft (11m)
long

Suchomimus

ACROCANTHOSAURUS
Cretaceous, 110 mya
North America
43ft (13m) long
Acrocanthosaurus had 1ft 5in-(43cm) long spines growing from its neck to its tail along its backbone. They may have had a skin "sail" stretched between them. *Acrocanthosaurus* was a fierce meat-eater with a big head, 4ft 6in (1.4m) long. Its jaws were filled with 68 serrated teeth, good for slicing through soft meat, but not for going through bone. Its arms ended in powerful hands which had three large, curved claws – well designed for capturing and holding on to its prey.

Closely related to *Spinosaurus*, and living at roughly the same time and in the same part of the world, was *Suchomimus*. It too had a "sail" on its back, though not as high. Also a fish-eater, *Suchomimus* had a 4ft- (1.2m-) long snout, inside which were about 100 pointed teeth. The teeth were razor-sharp and angled slightly backward, making it hard for a fish to slip from its mouth.

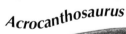
Acrocanthosaurus

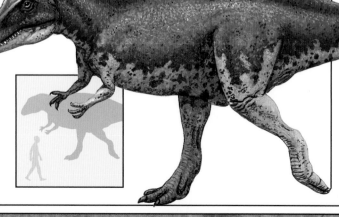

Suchomimus had short arms and its hands had three fingers. On one finger of each hand grew a sickle-like claw 1ft (30cm) long – the ideal "tool" to flick a fish out of the water, or simply impale it.

Spinosaurus

SPINOSAURUS

Cretaceous,
100 mya
Africa
49ft (15m) long

Spinosaurus was a giant meat-eater. It seems to have had a diet of fish, which it caught with its long jaws. On its back was a row of bony spines, each up to 6ft 6in (2m) long. They supported a skin "sail," which may have been brightly colored. The "sail" might have been used for display purposes, acting as a calling sign to a mate during courtship. It might also have frightened animals away, especially if *Spinosaurus* could change it to a warning color by "blushing" it red with blood. Another idea is that the "sail" controlled the animal's body temperature, trapping heat from the Sun to keep the dinosaur warm and, therefore, active.

IRRITATOR

Cretaceous, 100 mya
South America
26ft (8m) long

A spinosaur from South America, *Irritator* was also a fish-eater whose crocodile-like jaws were packed with hook-shaped teeth – ideal for snaring fish. So far only one skull has been found. It was discovered by amateur fossil hunters who used plaster of Paris to "restore" its broken snout. This irritated the experts so much they named the dinosaur *Irritator*! As the skull is so like that of *Spinosaurus* and *Suchomimus*, it is thought that *Irritator* looked like them too, and had a skin "sail" on its back.

Irritator

TEMPERATURE

If the "sails" on spinosaur backs were to control body heat, perhaps they absorbed the Sun's warmth first thing in the day. This would provide enough energy for the day ahead.

BARYONYX

The discovery of a new kind of meat-eating dinosaur is a major event, especially if its fossilized skeleton turns out to be almost complete. This is what happened in the case of *Baryonyx*, a previously unknown species of fish-eating dinosaur discovered in the south of England. Not only were almost all of its bones found, but even the remains of its final meal came to light.

LEAFY HABITAT

Baryonyx lived along the margins of rivers and pools, in a woodland flood plain where conifers, cycads, monkey puzzle trees, ferns and horsetails grew. *Baryonyx* shared this habitat with many other animals, such as the plant-eating *Iguanodon*, and the meat-eating *Megalosaurus*. Turtles and crocodiles lived in the water, and dragonflies flew in the air.

GIANT THUMB CLAW

Baryonyx *had three fingers on each hand. There was a long curved claw on its inside fingers (its thumbs). In a fully grown adult, the claw was 1ft 2in (35cm) long, and it was probably covered with a horny sheath, just like the claw of a bird. The name* Baryonyx *means "Heavy Claw."*

Claw on left thumb

LONG-NECKED CARNIVORE

Baryonyx was a meat-eater that walked on two legs. It had a narrow head and a long snout, like a crocodile. Its arms were strong and its fingers had curved claws. It had a long, straight neck, which was unusual for big carnivores – most had necks shaped like a letter S. Its tail was long and straight.

THE DISCOVERY

One of *Baryonyx*'s thumb claws was found in 1983 by an amateur fossil collector. He found it in a claypit in Surrey, England. That spring, scientists from London's Natural History Museum excavated the site, uncovering the fossilized bones of *Baryonyx*. Only its tail was missing.

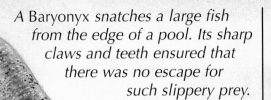

A Baryonyx snatches a large fish from the edge of a pool. Its sharp claws and teeth ensured that there was no escape for such slippery prey.

Name: *Baryonyx*
Lived: *125 million years ago*
Found: *Europe*
Length: *33ft (10m)*
Diet: *Fish, and possibly carrion*
Habitat: *Marshy, open woodland*

DIET OF FISH

When *Baryonyx* was excavated, the fossilized remains of its last meal were found within its stomach. Scientists identified teeth and scales from a species of fish called *Lepidotes*, a fish that grew to about 3ft 3in (1m) in length. Besides fish, *Baryonyx* might also have eaten carrion – meat from dead animals.

TOOTH-FILLED JAWS

Baryonyx had a long, slender skull. It ended in a spoon-shaped tip, which would have been useful for scooping up fish. Seen from the side, its upper jaw was S-shaped – modern fish-eating crocodiles also have jaws this shape. Its jaws were packed with 96 small, sharp teeth.

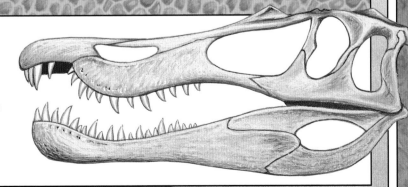

Meat-eating dinosaurs evolved many highly specialized features. Some, such as *Troodon*, became adapted to life in the far north of the world, where it was not only cold but where there were more hours of darkness than daylight. The ability to be able to see at night was a distinct advantage in the survival stakes. Other carnivores, such as *Avimimus*, grew into animals with many bird-like features – a sign that they were slowly evolving into a completely new kind of animal.

TROODON

Cretaceous, 70 million years ago
North America, Europe
6ft 6in (2m) long
A medium-sized carnivore, *Troodon* was a lightly-built dinosaur. With its long legs it was probably a fast runner, moving at speed after its prey, such as smaller reptiles and mammals. It may also have been an egg-eater, since its teeth have been found mixed up with shattered dinosaur eggs, suggesting they were part of its diet. Perhaps it also ate the defenseless hatchlings of other dinosaurs, raiding their nesting sites when the adults were not guarding their young.

SINORNITHOIDES

Cretaceous, 105 mya
Asia
3ft 6in (1.1m) long

Sinornithoides

Sinornithoides is one of the smallest meat-eating dinosaurs known – about the size of a turkey. Its long legs indicate it was a fast runner, and a large brain cavity inside its skull suggests it was an intelligent creature.

Sinornithoides had a compact body, and a long, whip-like tail that accounted for half its overall length. It probably ate small mammals and reptiles, as well as insects.

Troodon

ORNITHOLESTES

Jurassic, 150 mya
North America
6ft 6in (2m) long
Ornitholestes was an agile carnivore that lived in a forest habitat. It ate lizards, small mammals, and possibly the first birds which appeared in the late Jurassic period. It may also have been a carrion feeder, scavenging meat from the bodies of dead animals. *Ornitholestes* had a small head and its jaws contained sharp teeth. A bony crest grew on the top of its snout. It had a long, thin tail. As it ran, it held its tail straight behind it for balance. To change direction, *Ornitholestes* would have swung its tail to one side.

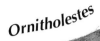

Ornitholestes

AVIMIMUS

Cretaceous,
80 mya
Asia
5ft (1.5m) long
Avimimus was a long-legged dinosaur that resembled a bird – but it was not a bird. Its head was bird-like, with a large brain, large eyes and a toothless beak. Its arms could be folded close to its body, like a bird folds its wings. Although no evidence for feathers has been found on *Avimimus*, some scientists believe it may have grown them on its arms – but it could not fly because its arms were too short for flight. *Avimimus* was probably an omnivore, eating both plants and meat, especially insects.

Avimimus

GOOD EYESIGHT

Troodon had large eyes, about 2in (5cm) across, which suggests it had good vision. It may have been a night hunter, able to detect its prey in the dark. Given that it lived in the far north of Canada and Russia, close to the Arctic Circle where winter daylight hours are short, keen eyesight would have been essential for survival.

OVIRAPTOR

This dinosaur was found in the 1920s on top of a nest of eggs. They were thought to belong to *Protoceratops*, a medium-sized herbivore. It was decided the new dinosaur was stealing the *Protoceratops'* eggs, so it was named *Oviraptor*, meaning "Egg Thief." Then, in the 1990s, more eggs were found, similar to those discovered in the 1920s. Because one had a baby *Oviraptor* inside it, it was realized the dinosaur was not an egg-stealer after all. Instead, *Oviraptor* had been found sitting on a nest of its own eggs, incubating them until they hatched.

OVIRAPTOR SKULL

Oviraptor's skull was small and lightweight, with large holes for its eyes. The most striking feature of its skull was a tall, bony crest which grew above its nose. The crest was probably covered in a layer of horn. Its toothless beak was very much like that of a bird.

A group of Oviraptor *dinosaurs at their breeding ground, tending to their nests of carefully arranged eggs.*